**STATE OF VERMONT
DEPARTMENT OF LIBRARIES
REGIONAL LIBRARY
RD 2   BOX 244
ST. JOHNSBURY, VT 05819**

D1790858

Take a trip to INDONESIA

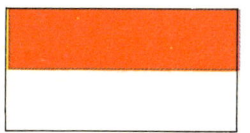

Keith Lye
General Editor
Henry Pluckrose

Franklin Watts
London   New York   Sydney   Toronto

Facts about Indonesia

Area:
1,904,569 sq. km
(735,398 sq. miles)

Population:
147,490,000 (1980)

Capital:
Djakarta

Largest cities:
Djakarta (4,576,000);
Surubaya (1,556,000);
Bandung (1,202,000);
Semarang (647,000)

Official language:
Bahasa Indonesia

Main religions:
Islam (80 per cent),
Christianity, Hinduism,
Buddhism

Main exports:
Oil, coffee, rubber,
palm-oil, tin, tea,
tobacco

Currency:
Rupiah

Franklin Watts Limited
12a Golden Square
London W1

Franklin Watts Inc.
387 Park Avenue South
New York N.Y. 10016

ISBN: UK Edition 0 86313 091 7
ISBN: US Edition 0-531-04940-X
Library of Congress Catalog Card No:
84-51806

© Franklin Watts Limited 1985

Text Editor: Brenda Williams
Maps: Tony Payne
Design: Mushroom Production
Stamps: Stanley Gibbons Limited
Photographs: Zefa; Colorpix/Ron Carter,
3, 6, 12, 15, 16, 24, 25, 28, 30, 31;
J. Allan Cash, 5, 11, 13, 14, 21
Front and Back Covers: Zefa

Typeset by Ace Filmsetting Ltd,
Frome, Somerset
Printed in Hong Kong

Indonesia is an island nation in south-eastern Asia. In the west it includes Sumatra. It also includes Kalimantan (part of Borneo), Java and Sulawesi. Irian Jaya (part of New Guinea) is in the east. There are also 3,000 more smaller islands. The town of Prapat is in Sumatra.

Only China, India, Russia and the USA have more people than Indonesia. About two-thirds of Indonesia's people live on the island of Java. In central Java there is a huge Buddhist temple, the Borobudur.

About 20 out of every 100 people in Indonesia live in cities and towns. Seven of the country's ten largest cities are on Java. Jogjakarta is in central Java. It is Indonesia's tenth largest city.

Most Indonesians have Malay or Polynesian ancestors. Bahasa Indonesian means Indonesian language and is the country's official language. It is based on Malay but also has some Dutch and local words. These girls live in Sumatra.

About 25 languages and 250 dialects are spoken in Indonesia. In the inland forests of Kalimantan live people called Dyaks. There are about 50 different groups of Dyak peoples. People of Malay and Chinese origin live on the coasts.

The picture shows some stamps and money used in Indonesia. The main unit of currency is the rupiah, which is divided into 100 sen.

Irian Jaya is in east Indonesia. It shares the island of New Guinea with another country, Papua New Guinea, and most of its people are Papuans. But few people live in Irian Jaya. Parts of it have never been explored.

Indonesia has 167 active volcanoes, more than any other country. Of these, 77 have erupted in historic times. This is Mount Batur, a volcano on Bali. West of Java is Krakatoa, which erupted with an enormous volcanic explosion in 1883.

Djakarta is in north-west Java. It is Indonesia's capital. Here are the country's government buildings and the President's palace. The Dutch first ruled Indonesia in 1602, through the Dutch East India Company. In 1799 the Dutch government took over.

The independent Republic of Indonesia was set up in 1949, after four years of bitter fighting between Indonesians and their Dutch rulers. Djakarta's old city hall, built in 1710, recalls the days of Dutch rule.

Indonesia's third largest city is Bandung, on Java. Bicycle-driven vehicles called becaks are still often used for transport.

Horsecabs are another way to travel on the small island of Bali. This island east of Java is known for its great beauty. It is also famous for its many Hindu temples.

Rice is the chief food crop in Indonesia. Flooded paddy fields in Bali are being levelled so that young lowland, or swamp rice plants can be brought from nurseries for planting.

Rice is harvested when the golden heads of the plants hang downwards. About 58 out of every 100 people in Indonesia work on farms. Only 12 out of 100 work in industry.

Dense forests cover about two-thirds of Indonesia, and so timber is an important product. Here, it is being exported through Djakarta. Rubber is another forest product.

Tobacco is grown in Indonesia. This plantation is in Java. Coffee, palm-oil and tea are other crops grown mainly for export.

Fish is an important food for many Indonesians. Here, a fisherman casts his net in the shallow waters off western Bali.

Oil is Indonesia's most valuable export. Most of it comes from Sumatra, Kalimantan and Java. At this oil pumping station in southern Sumatra, natural gas is burned off.

Indonesia produces some tin, bauxite, copper and other metals. But most of its minerals have not yet been used. Sulphur is being dug out of this volcanic crater in Java.

Most of the country has a hot, wet climate. The southern islands have a dry season between May and October. More tourists are visiting Indonesia, especially Bali, which has modern hotels. But Indonesia is poor compared to western countries.

Four out of every five Indonesians are Muslims and follow the religion of Islam. Muslims in the river port of Samarinda, east Kalimantan, worship at this mosque.

Bali is the only island where Islam is not the chief religion. Most people on Bali are Hindus. In this picture, Hindu dancers are performing a temple play.

Children in cities, such as these in Jogjakarta, have the best chances of going to a government or private school. There are not enough teachers, schools or books for all of the country's children.

Village schools often teach adults who never went to school when they were young. This school is in the countryside of Irian Jaya. More than 30 out of every 100 adults in Indonesia cannot read or write.

There are many open-air markets in Indonesia. In these busy, noisy places, women buy fresh fruits and vegetables for their families.

Gamelan orchestras are popular in Indonesia. They use mostly percussion instruments, such as xylophones and drums. Music is used in religious ceremonies and also for dancing and puppet plays.

Weavers in Bali make beautiful silk cloth. Other Indonesian crafts include wood carving, silverwork and batik. Batik is an old way of making patterns on cloth, by using wax to cover areas not to be dyed.

The number of people in Indonesia is growing quickly, and Java is a crowded island. But the country is changing as industries grow up in the fast-growing cities, such as the busy capital of Djakarta.

Index

Bali 15–16, 20, 23, 30
Bandung 14
Borobudur 4

Climate 23
Crafts 30

Djakarta 12–13, 18, 31
Dutch rule 12–13
Dyaks 7

Education 26–27

Farming 16–19
Fishing 20
Forests 18

Gamelan orchestra 29

Hinduism 15, 25
History 12–13

Industry 21–22, 31
Irian Jaya 3, 10, 27
Islam 24

Java 3–5, 11, 14, 19, 21–22, 31
Jogjakarta 5, 26

Kalimantan 3, 7, 21, 24
Krakatoa 11

Languages 6

Mining 22
Money 8
Mount Batur 11
Music 29

Oil 21

Papuans 10
Prapat (Sumatra) 3

Religion 4, 15, 24–25
Rice 16–17

Schools 26–27
Silk weaving 30
Stamps 8
Sulawesi 3
Sumatra 3, 6, 21

Tobacco 19
Tourism 23
Transport 14–15

Volcanoes 11, 22